For Mark "Mega" Guppy

The Teacher and Student Method

Drum Set Studies

Exercise Book One

CONTENTS

CONTENTS

A NOTE TO TEACHERS

This isn't an ordinary method book. The **Teacher and Student Method** series of books have been written with you, the instructor, in mind. There are many self-teaching and highly detailed instructional books on the market, but none have been designed so that you can teach using your own systems and methods.

You will find that, throughout this book, certain pages have been set aside so that you can teach your students the basics. The **Teacher's Notes** pages contain a blank space to be used like a blackboard, as well as some empty manuscript for transcribing some of your own ideas and exercises (or even song samples). Make sure that you check ahead of the **Teacher's Notes** pages to see what the next subject may be, and then you can teach your student until they understand it… and nothing else! After all, not all of your students will require the same level of demonstration and explanation of the exercises. These books are purely dedicated to giving the student a rigorous run through all of the skills and techniques they need to know, providing them with a rich and resourceful insight into the art of drumming. And you still get to focus on teaching!

Do you have issues with your student not practicing enough? While this may be frustrating from the standpoint of a teacher, children (and adults) are often too busy with work, recreation, and other daily activities to really find the time to dedicate themselves to their music the way you would like them to. While it is never a good thing to skip on practicing, the **Teacher and Student Method** covers each skill in great detail, allowing the student to grasp a thorough understanding of the many areas of drumming covered in this book. Of course, that should never mean that your student ever gets a free ride!

A NOTE TO STUDENTS

Welcome to the **Teacher and Student Method** series of books. You have just purchased (or stolen) a comprehensive and progressive teaching aid that will help you to accomplish your dream of becoming a drummer. Now, drummers may be the butt of all jokes from the other members of the band, but let's face it… they need us! These books will allow you and your teacher to cover all of the skills needed in becoming a "Stickman". There are pages in this book that are dedicated to your instructor, which will allow them to teach you the basics their own way, until you understand what you need to know and can move on. No longer do you have to read through pages of boring notes and demonstrations, most of which are unnecessary. Once you get the picture, it's time to play and do what you were born to do… Good luck!

ABOUT THIS BOOK

Thank you for bringing your (good) self to **The Teacher and Student Method Drum Set Studies Exercise Book 1**. This is the first in a series of books that will extensively cover all areas of playing the drum set, as well as touching on snare basics. However, if you wish to explore the snare drum or drumline in greater detail, there are a number of good instructional books that will help you along the way:

Savage Rudimental Workshop by Matt Savage – Warner Brothers Pub. (2001)

Alfred's Drum Method books 1 & 2 by Sandy Feldstein and Dave Black – Alfred Pub. Company (2006)

Stick Control for the Snare Drummer by George Lawrence Stone – George B. Stone & Son, Inc. (1998)

A Fresh Approach to the Snare Drum by Mark Wessels – Mark Wessels Pub. (2006)

ABOUT THE AUTHOR

Owen Liversidge graduated from Leeds University, England, with a degree in Popular Music Studies, in 2000. He has played drum set since he was 17, performing with numerous bands and projects across the UK. Since leaving College, Owen has been living in Atlanta, GA, where he has been teaching drums since 2002. He was inspired to write this book by the apparent lack of comprehensive instructional materials, which allowed the student and teacher to work together towards a common goal... to produce a complete and seasoned drummer!

The only thing missing from this book, which Owen wanted to include, is songs. Unfortunately, the Copyright and Publishing laws forbid any printed versions of a released song or album. However, there are a couple of sites on the internet where you can download and print song transcriptions for the drum set (**drumscore.com** and **onlinedrummer.com**). It is very important—not to mention, fun—for the student to learn how to play songs, preferably by playing along with the recording. This is essential for the development, timing, and musicianship of the drummer-in-training. Luckily, we can also find a small collection of books with songs:

FastTrack Drum Songbook (Level 1, books 1 & 2; Level 2, book 1) by Hal Leonard Corp. – Hal Leonard Corp. (1997-1999)

Classic Rock Drummers (The Way they Play) by Ken Micallef – Backbeat Books (2007)

The Beatles Drum Collection by The Beatles – Hal Leonard Corp. (2000)

DRUMSET COMPONENTS

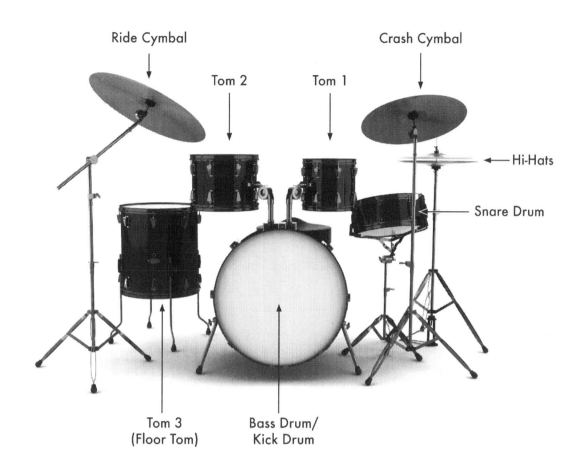

Ride Cymbal

Crash Cymbal

Tom 2

Tom 1

Hi-Hats

Snare Drum

Tom 3
(Floor Tom)

Bass Drum/
Kick Drum

DRUMSET NOTATION

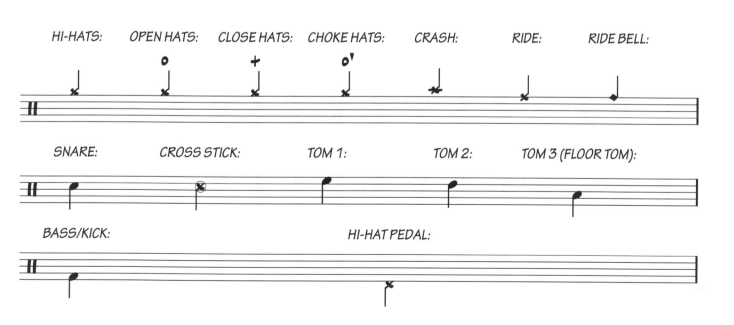

HI-HATS: OPEN HATS: CLOSE HATS: CHOKE HATS: CRASH: RIDE: RIDE BELL:

SNARE: CROSS STICK: TOM 1:   TOM 2:   TOM 3 (FLOOR TOM):

BASS/KICK: HI-HAT PEDAL:

NOTES AND RESTS (IN CONTEXT)

CLEF: Drums and percussion (unpitched) use the **Neutral Clef**

TIME SIGNATURE: The top number indicates the amount of beats (counts) in a measure
The bottom number indicates what note value each beat receives -
(in this case, **1/4** note)

WHOLE NOTE:
1 (2) (3) (4)

WHOLE NOTE REST:
(1) (2) (3) (4)

HALF NOTE:
1 (2) 3 (4)

HALF NOTE REST:
(1) (2) (3) (4)

QUARTER NOTE:
1 2 3 4

QUARTER NOTE REST:
(1) (2) (3) (4)

EIGHTH NOTE:
1 & 2 & 3 & 4 &

EIGHTH NOTE REST:
(1) (&) (2) (&) (3) (&) (4) (&)

SIXTEENTH NOTE:
1 e & a 2 e & a 3 e & a 4 e & a

SIXTEENTH NOTE REST:
(1) (e) (&) (a) (2) (e) (&) (a) (3) (e) (&) (a) (4) (e) (&) (a)

EIGHTH NOTE TRIPLET:
1 & a 2 & a 3 & a 4 & a
3   3   3   3

EIGHTH NOTE TRIPLET REST:
(1) (&) (a) (2) (&) (a) (3) (&) (a) (4) (&) (a)
3   3   3   3

REFERENCES

1   **BAR NUMBER:** Indicates the number of the current measure

~~**SINGLE BAR (OR MEASURE)**~~

SINGLE BARLINE: Indicates the split between measures on the stave

ENDING BARLINE: Indicates the end of the current piece of music

START REPEAT: Indicates the beginning of a repeated section or passage

END REPEAT: Indicates the end of a repeated section or passage

SINGLE BAR REPEAT: Repeat the previous measure

DOUBLE BAR REPEAT: Repeat the previous two measures

ACCENT: Play the note or expression louder

FERMATA (PAUSE): Play the note or expression to a cue or agreed rest time

DAL SEGNO: Repeat from this symbol when you see *D.S.* or *D.S al Coda*

CODA: Jump from one of these symbols to the next after playing from *Dal Segno* in *D.S. al Coda*, or the beginning from *D.C. al Coda*

1st ENDING: Play through this section of music the first time

Cresc. **CRESCENDO:** Gradually increase the volume

Dim. **DIMINUENDO:** Gradually decrease the volume

TEACHER'S NOTES - LEVEL 1

"The rhythm is in your blood" - African Proverb

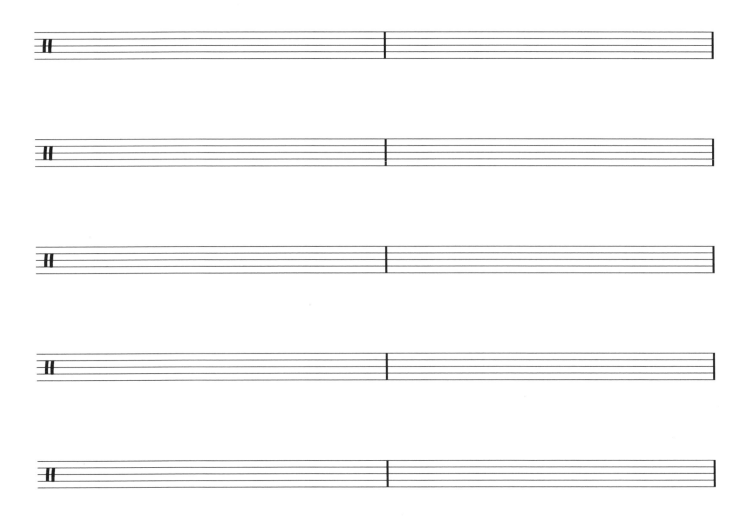

EIGHTH NOTE STICKING EXERCISES

Beginner - Play each exercise with a gradually increasing tempo

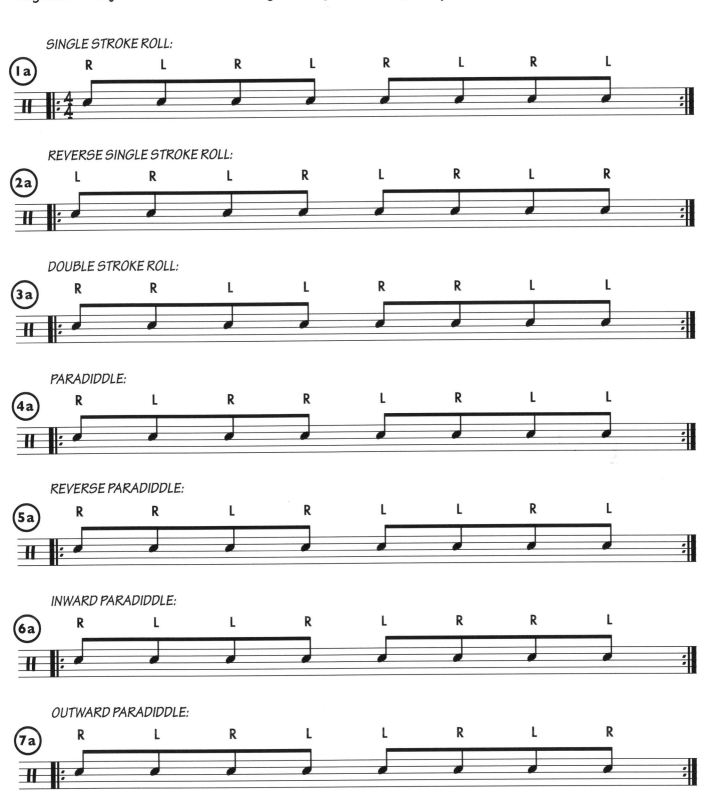

DRUM SET WARMUPS: SYNCHRONIZATION

Beginner - Play each exercise four times, aiming for accuracy

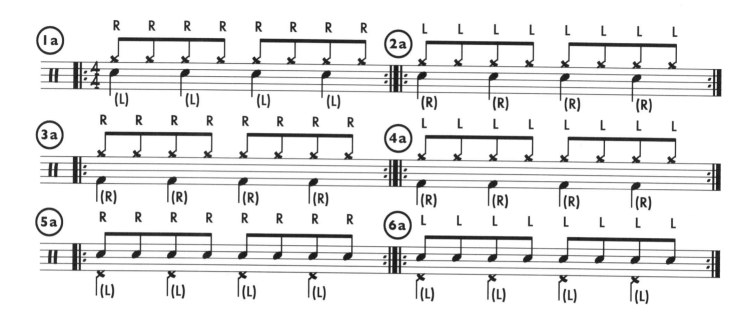

DRUM SET WARMUPS: SYNCOPATION

Beginner - Play each exercise with a gradually increasing tempo

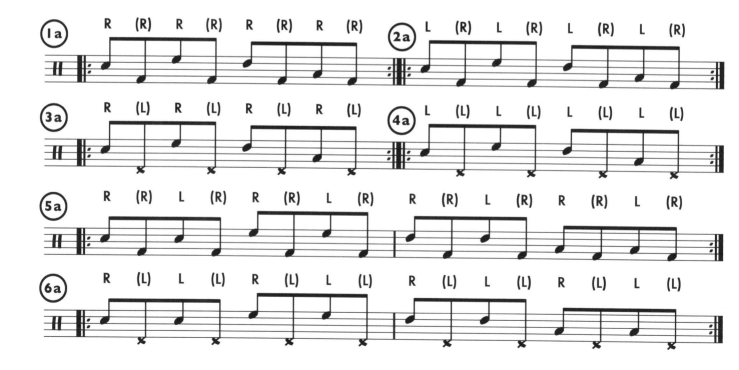

BEGINNING RHYTHM EXERCISES

Beginner - Play each exercise four times
Advanced - Play all sixteen exercises consecutively without repeats

EIGHTH NOTE BEATS

Beginner - Play each exercise four times
Advanced - Play all sixteen exercises consecutively without repeats

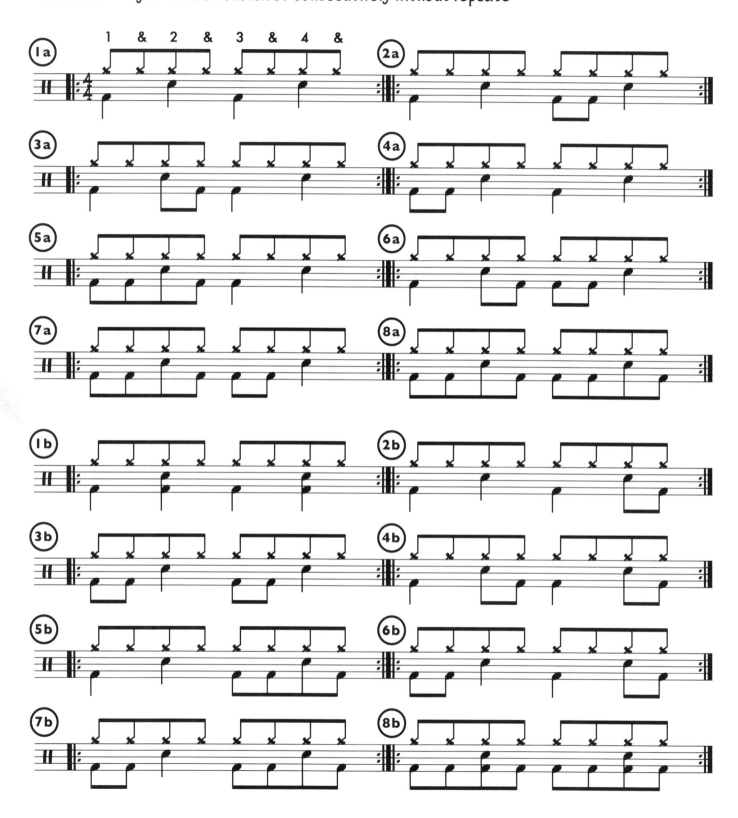

 ©2013 Owen Liversidge • Teacher and Student Publications

TEACHER'S NOTES - LEVEL 2

"You only get better by playing" - Buddy Rich

BEGINNING RHYTHM EXERCISES WITH RESTS

Beginner - Play each exercise four times
Advanced - Play all sixteen exercises consecutively without repeats

EIGHTH NOTE BEATS WITH RESTS

Beginner - Play each exercise four times
Advanced - Play all fourteen exercises consecutively without repeats

EIGHTH NOTE COMBINATION BEATS (WITH RIDE)

Beginner - Play each exercise four times
Advanced - Play all eight exercises consecutively without repeats

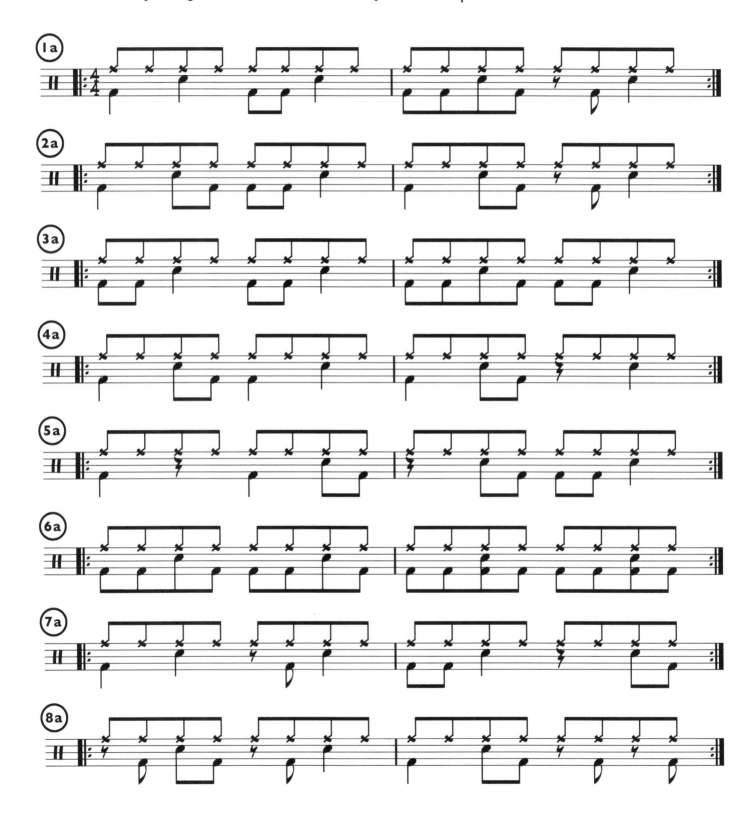

EIGHTH NOTE BEATS WITH DOUBLE SNARES

Beginner - Play each exercise four times
Advanced - Play all four exercises consecutively without repeats

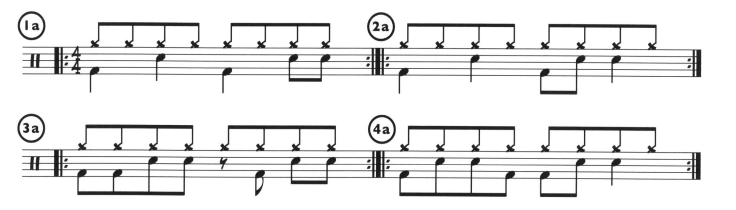

EIGHTH NOTE BEATS WITH ADDED CRASHES

Beginner - Play each exercise four times
Advanced - Play all eight exercises consecutively without repeats

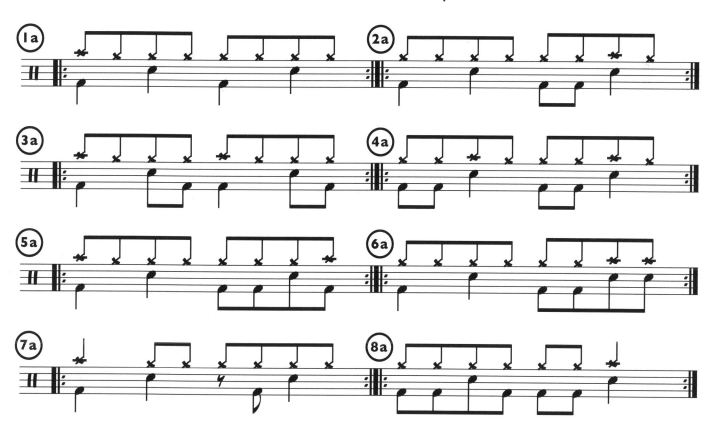

EIGHTH NOTE FILLS

Beginner - Play each exercise four times
Advanced - Play all eight exercises consecutively without repeats

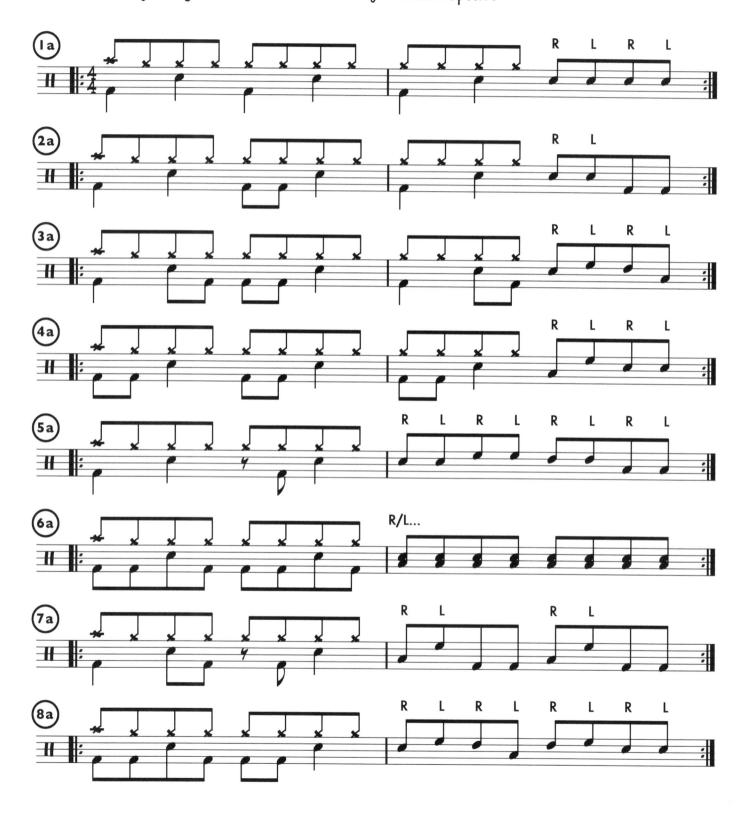

EIGHTH NOTE FILLS: CREATE YOUR OWN

Beginner - With your teacher, create your own eighth note fills using the same beats

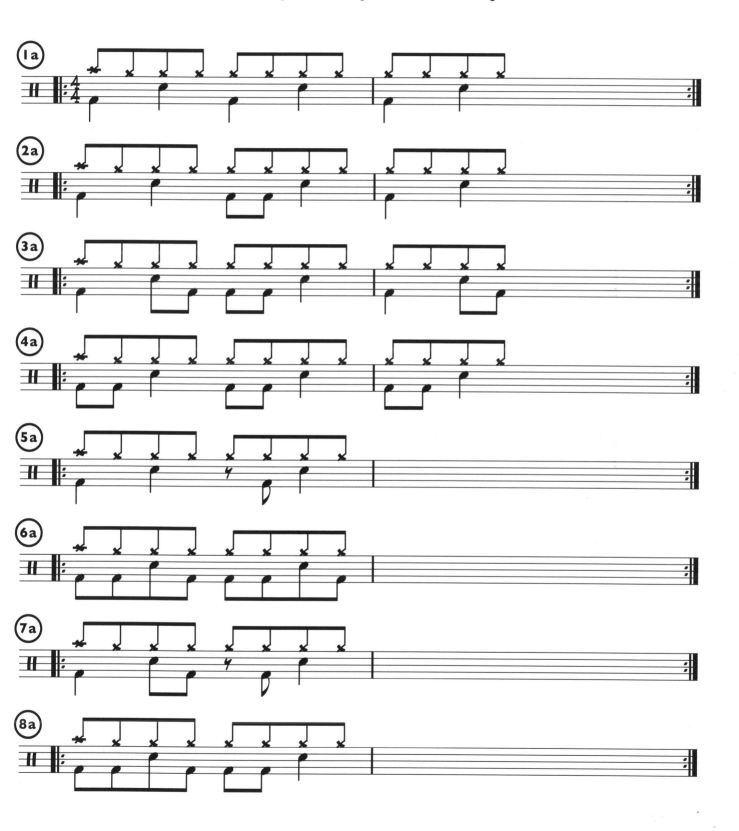

HALF-TIME BEATS (WITH CROSS STICKS)

Beginner - Play each exercise four times
Advanced - Play all six exercises consecutively without repeats

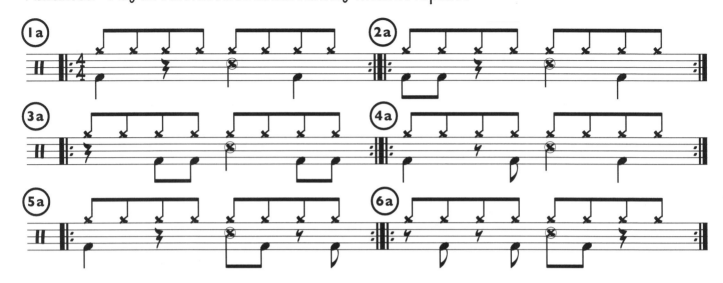

EXPLORING STYLES: THE LATIN "BOSSA NOVA"

Beginner - Play each exercise four times

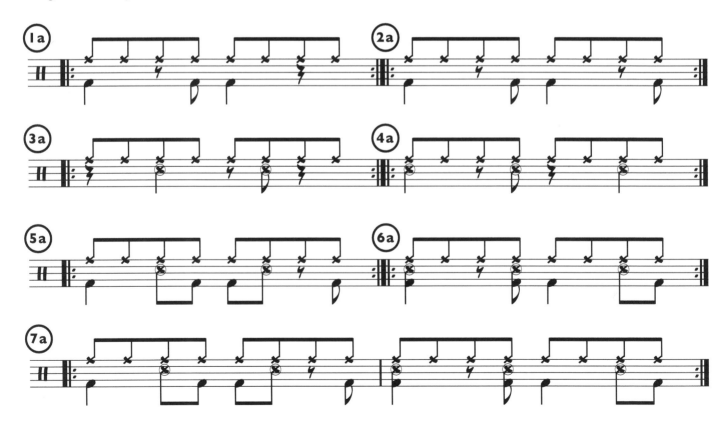

INTRODUCING FLAMS

Beginner - Play each exercise four times

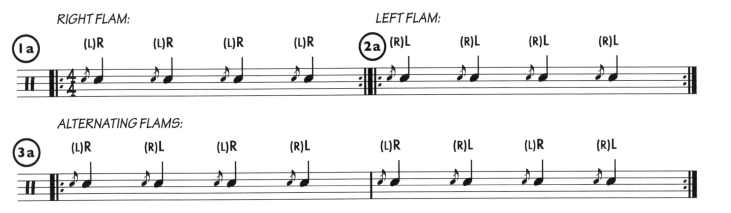

FLAMS AS FILLS

*Try using your favorite flam, then mix it up

Beginner - Play each exercise four times
Advanced - Play all four exercises consecutively without repeats

TEACHER'S NOTES - LEVEL 3

"Eat drums" - Animal

SIXTEENTH NOTE RHYTHM EXERCISES

Beginner - Play each exercise four times
Advanced - Play all sixteen exercises consecutively without repeats

SIXTEENTH NOTE BEATS

Beginner - Play each exercise four times
Advanced - Play all sixteen exercises consecutively without repeats

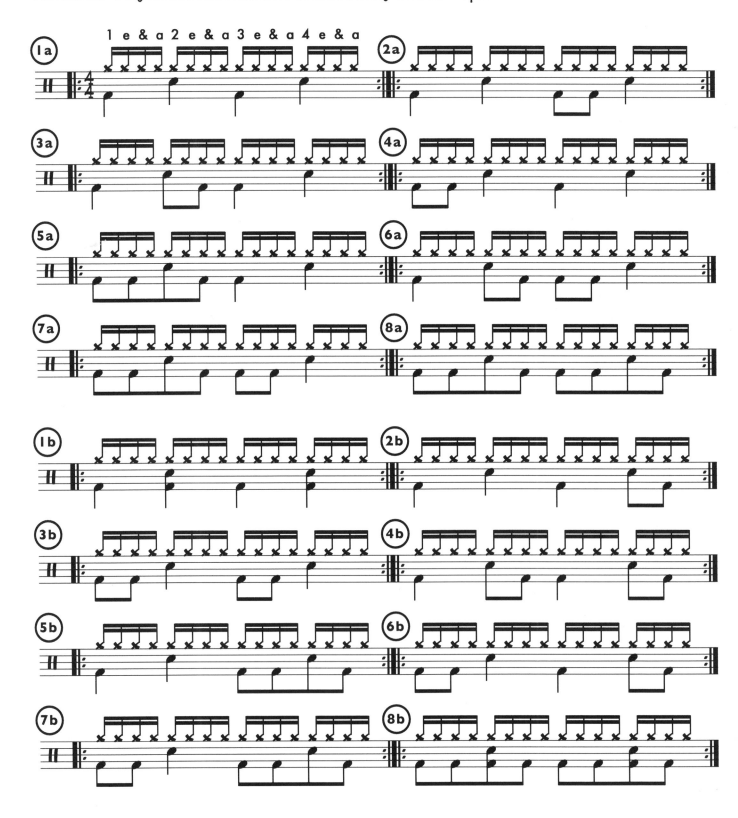

SIXTEENTH NOTE BEATS WITH RESTS

Beginner - Play each exercise four times
Advanced - Play all fourteen exercises consecutively without repeats

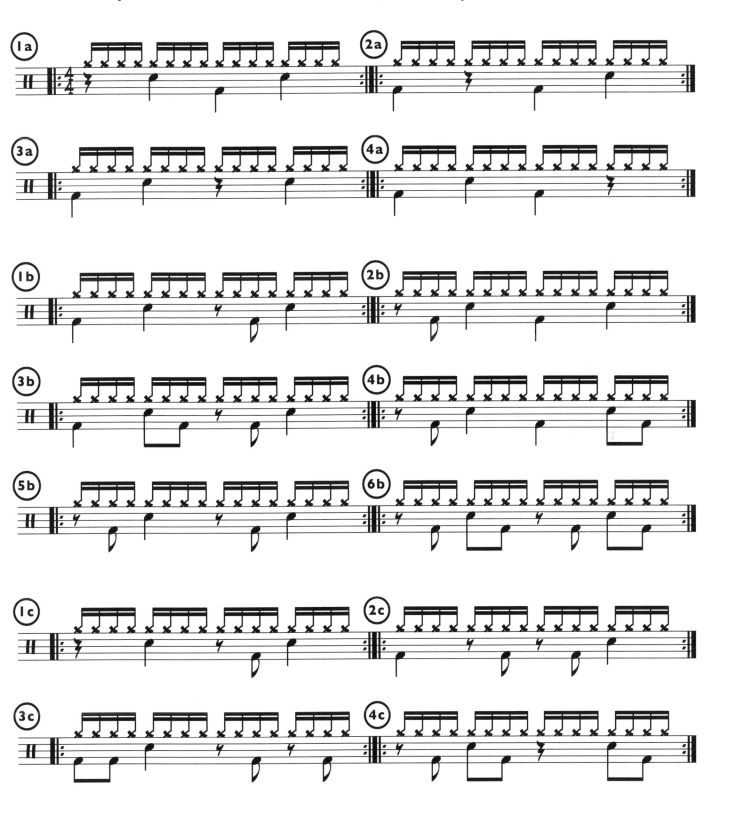

SIXTEENTH NOTE BEATS WITH DOUBLE SNARES

Beginner - Play each exercise four times
Advanced - Play all four exercises consecutively without repeats

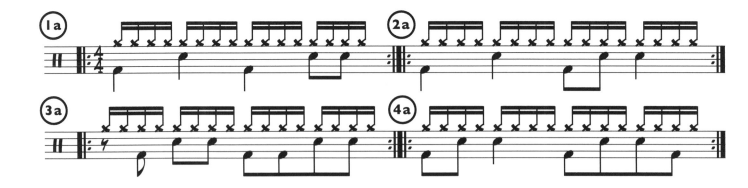

BAR REPEATS AND ALTERNATE ENDINGS

Beginner - Play entire exercise regarding the bar repeats and alternate endings

©2013 Owen Liversidge • Teacher and Student Publications

SIXTEENTH NOTE FILLS

Beginner - Play each exercise four times
Advanced - Play all eight exercises consecutively without repeats

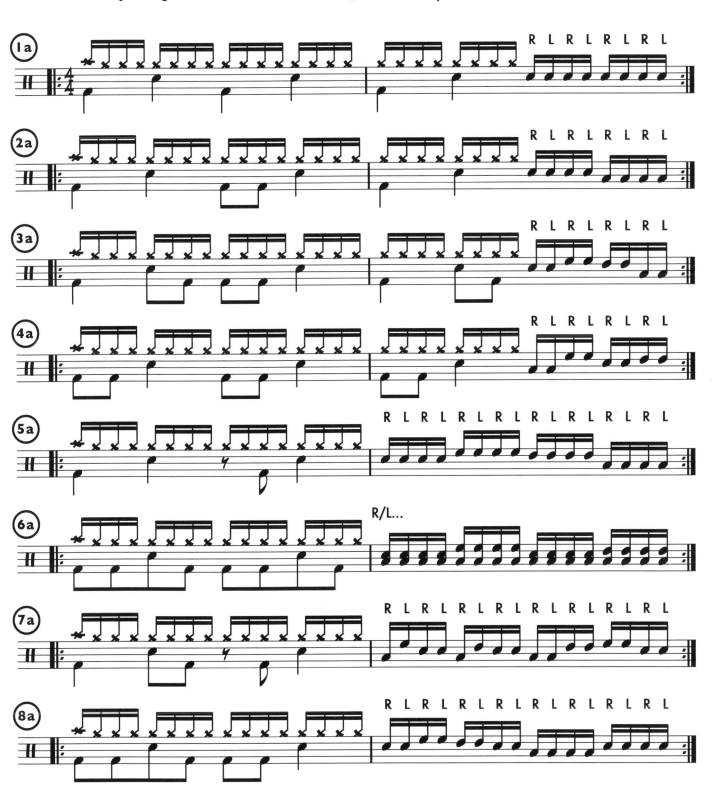

SIXTEENTH NOTE FILLS: CREATE YOUR OWN

Beginner - With your teacher, create your own sixteenth note fills using the same beats

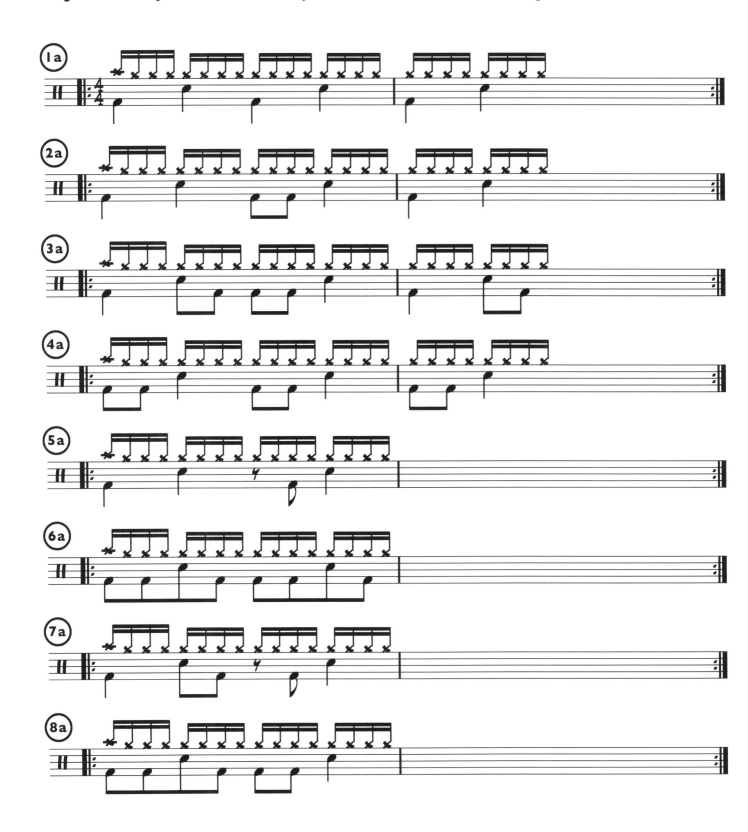

SIXTEENTH NOTE ENDURANCE EXERCISES

Beginner - Play each exercise as long as possible, gradually increasing the tempo
Advanced - Play all four exercises consecutively without repeats

SIXTEENTH NOTE DRUM SET EXERCISES

Beginner - Play each exercise as long as possible, gradually increasing the tempo
Advanced - Play all eight exercises consecutively without repeats

FOURS:

TWOS:

SINGLES:

ALTERNATING SIXTEENTH NOTE BASS PATTERNS

Beginner - Play each exercise four times
Advanced - Play all four exercises consecutively without repeats

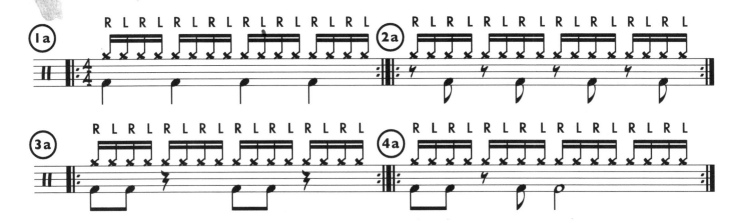

USING NUMBER CELLS TO CREATE FILLS

Beginner - Play each fill four times as an example, then create your own on next page
Advanced - Play all six exercises consecutively without repeats

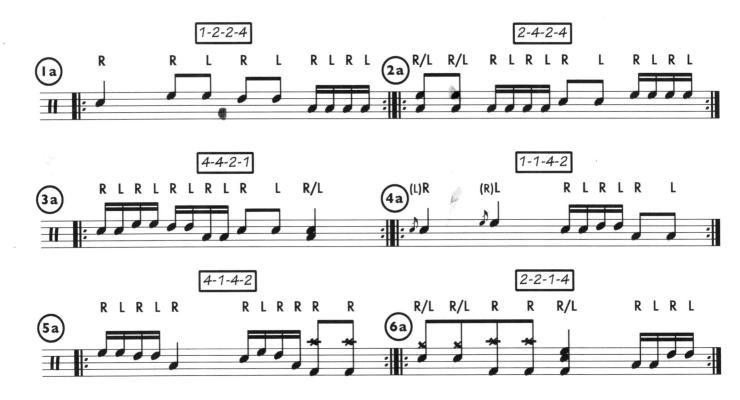

©2013 Owen Liversidge • Teacher and Student Publications

TEACHER'S NOTES - LEVEL 4

"Drummers don't write - or, at least, that's what everyone believes" - Tony Williams

*Create your own fills using a chosen number cell

1-2-4-4		

BEGINNING ACCENTED RHYTHMS

Beginner - Play each exercise four times (bass drum optional)
Advanced - Play all fourteen exercises consecutively without repeats

DYNAMICS

pp = Pianissimo (very soft)

p = Piano (soft)

mp = Mezzo Piano (moderately soft)

mf = Mezzo Forte (moderately loud)

f = Forte (loud)

ff = Fortissimo (very loud)

Beginner - Play each exercise four times

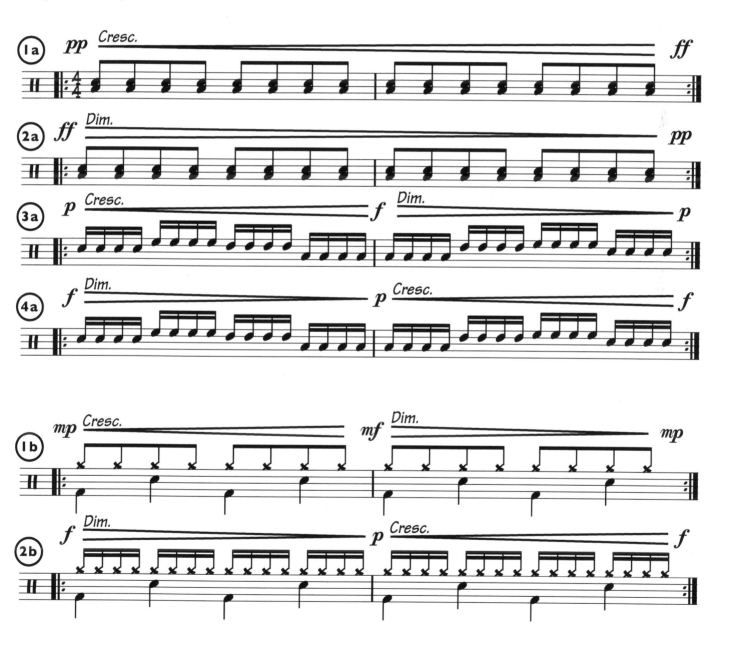

ACCENTS WITH HI-HAT

Beginner - Play each exercise four times, with shoulder/tip (Moeller Technique) on hi-hats

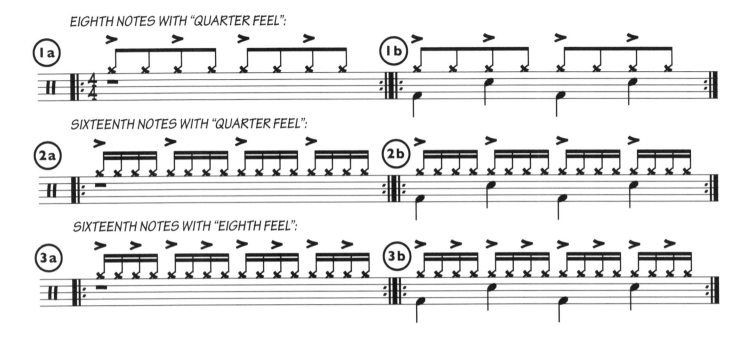

EIGHTH NOTES WITH "QUARTER FEEL":

SIXTEENTH NOTES WITH "QUARTER FEEL":

SIXTEENTH NOTES WITH "EIGHTH FEEL":

ACCENTS WITH RIDE (USING BELL)

Beginner - Play each exercise four times, using shoulder on bell for accents

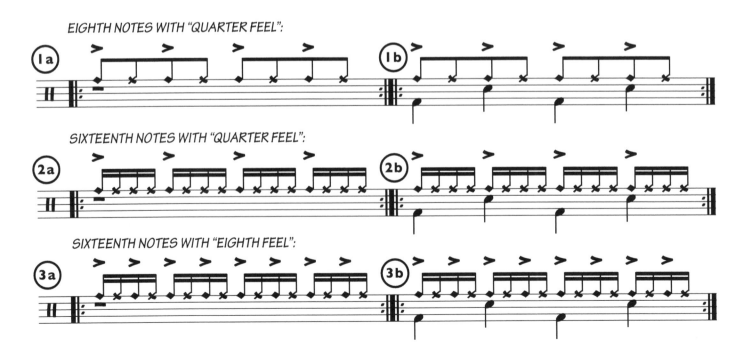

EIGHTH NOTES WITH "QUARTER FEEL":

SIXTEENTH NOTES WITH "QUARTER FEEL":

SIXTEENTH NOTES WITH "EIGHTH FEEL":

MUSICAL STYLES: ROCK 'N' ROLL (WITH PEDAL)

Beginner - Play each exercise four times

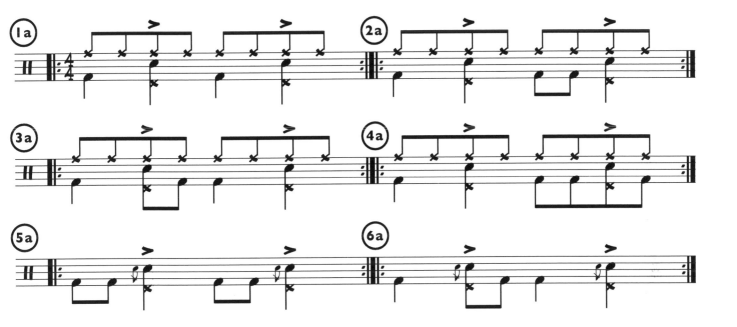

MUSICAL STYLES: ROCK & POP BEATS

Beginner - Play each exercise four times

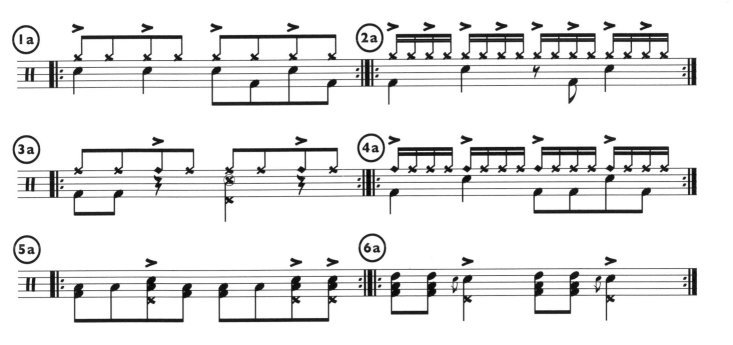

TEACHER'S NOTES - LEVEL 5

"Become the best musician that you can because that is your product - your own personal musicianship" - Steve Smith

QUARTER NOTE BEATS

Beginner - Play each exercise four times
Advanced - Play all sixteen exercises consecutively without repeats

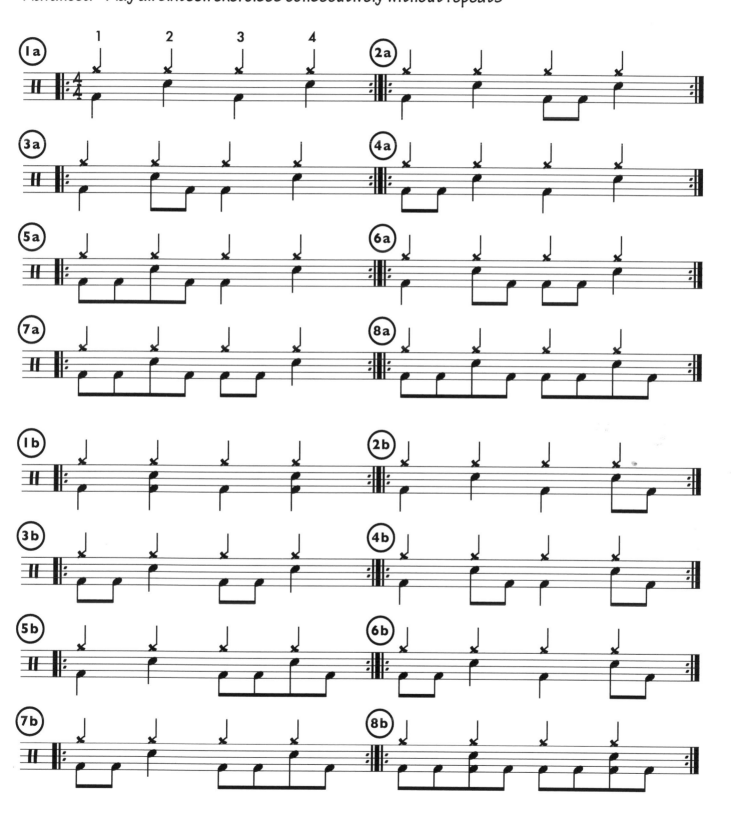

QUARTER NOTE BEATS WITH RESTS

Beginner - Play each exercise four times
Advanced - Play all fourteen exercises consecutively without repeats

QUARTER NOTE BEATS WITH DOUBLE SNARES

Beginner - Play each exercise four times
Advanced - Play all four exercises consecutively without repeats

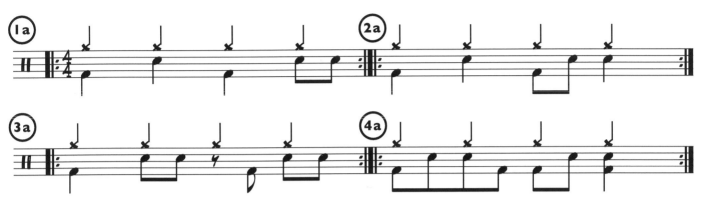

INTRODUCING LINEAR TIME PLAYING

Beginner - Play each exercise as long as possible, gradually increasing the tempo
Advanced - Play all four exercises consecutively without repeats

EIGHTH BEATS WITH SNARE DISPLACEMENT

Beginner - Play each exercise four times
Advanced - Play all sixteen exercises consecutively without repeats

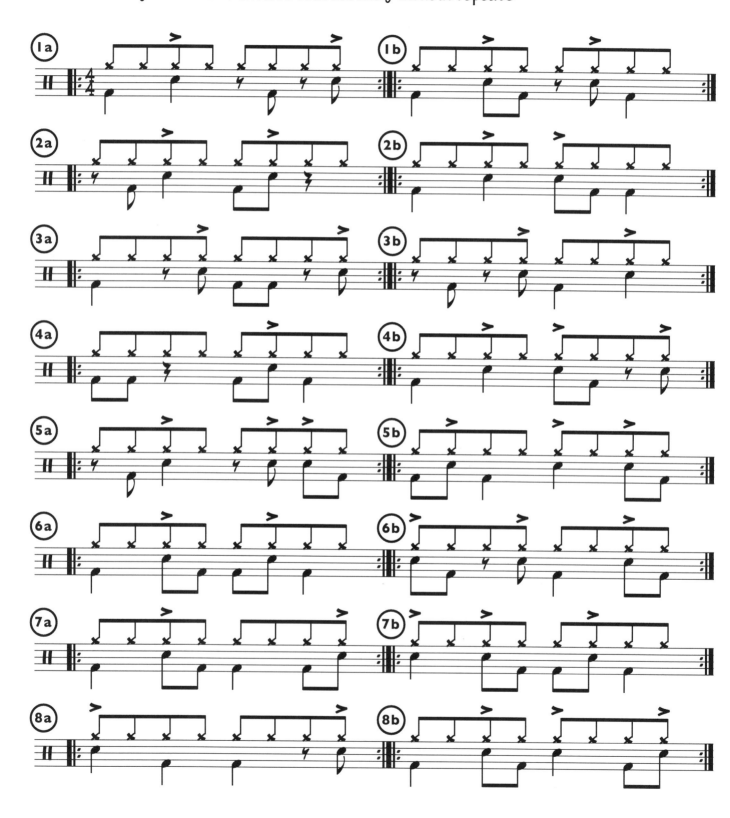

 ©2013 Owen Liversidge • Teacher and Student Publications

TEACHER'S NOTES - LEVEL 6

"I do not allow myself to take any negative comment in a personal way"
- Johnny Rabb

EIGHTH NOTE BEATS OPEN HI-HAT

Beginner - Play each exercise four times
Advanced - Play all fourteen exercises consecutively without repeats

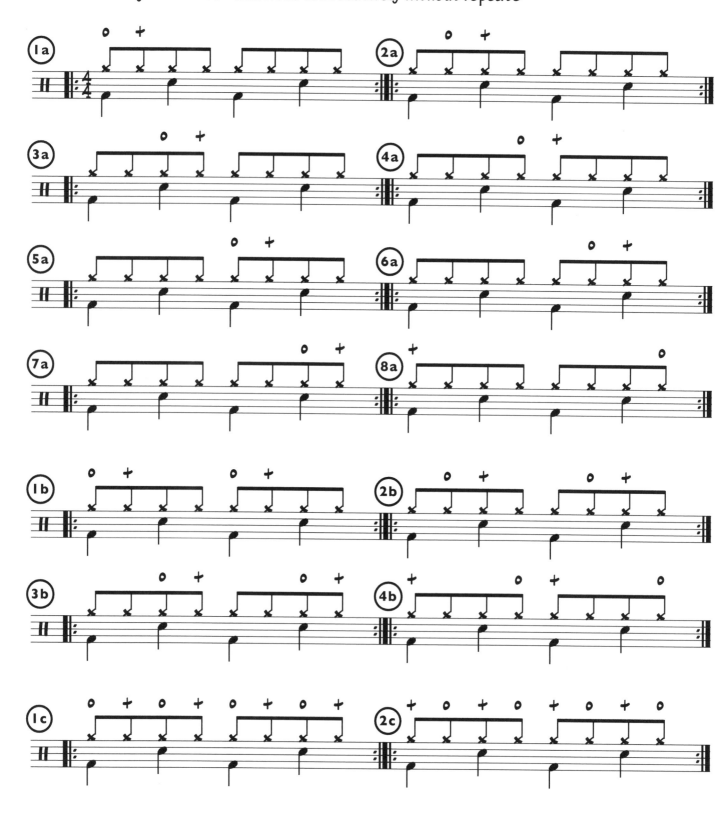

EIGHTH BEATS OPEN HI-HAT BASS COMBOS

Beginner - Play each exercise four times, practicing the basic beat first
Advanced - Play all eight exercises consecutively without repeats

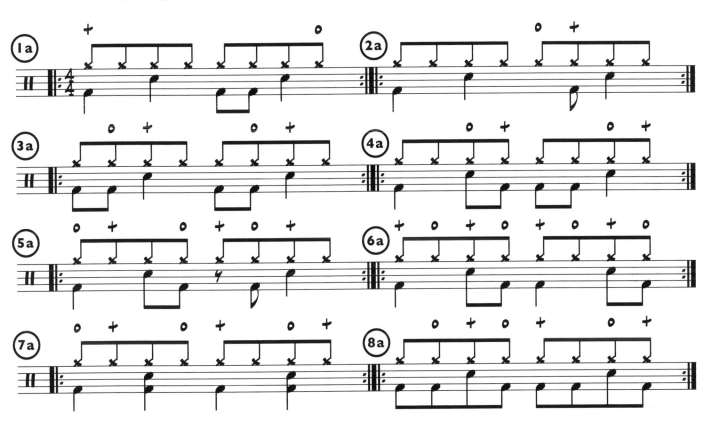

QUARTER BEATS OPEN HI-HAT BASS COMBOS

Beginner - Play each exercise four times
Advanced - Play all four exercises consecutively without repeats

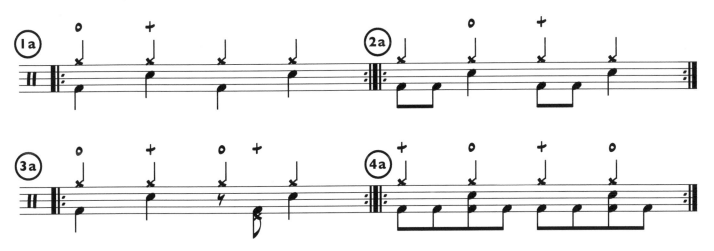

OPEN HI-HAT FILLS (WITH CHOKES)

Beginner - Play each exercise four times
Advanced - Play all seven exercises consecutively without repeats

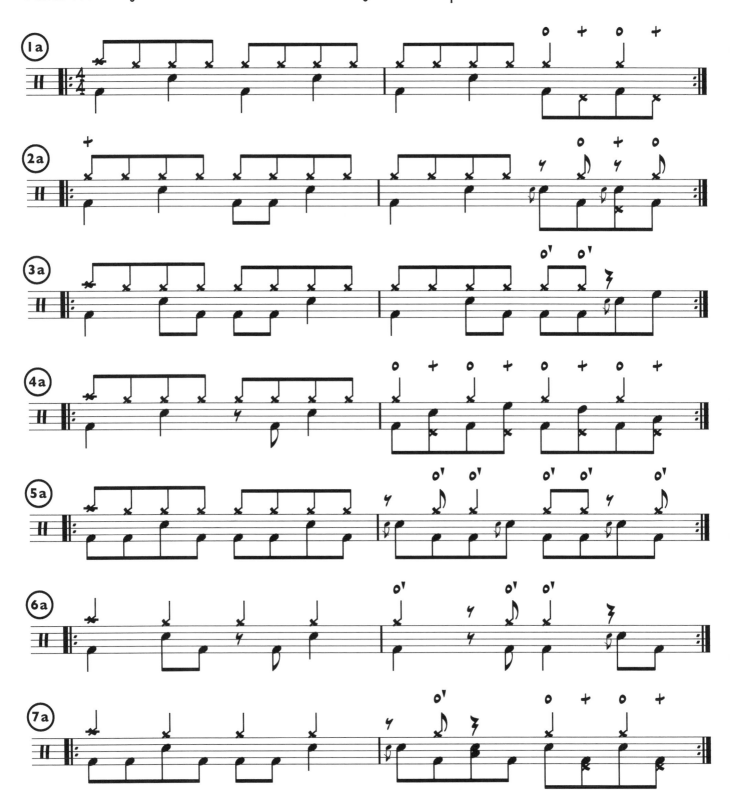

OPEN HI-HAT FILLS: CREATE YOUR OWN

Beginner - With your teacher, create your own open hi-hat fills using the same beats

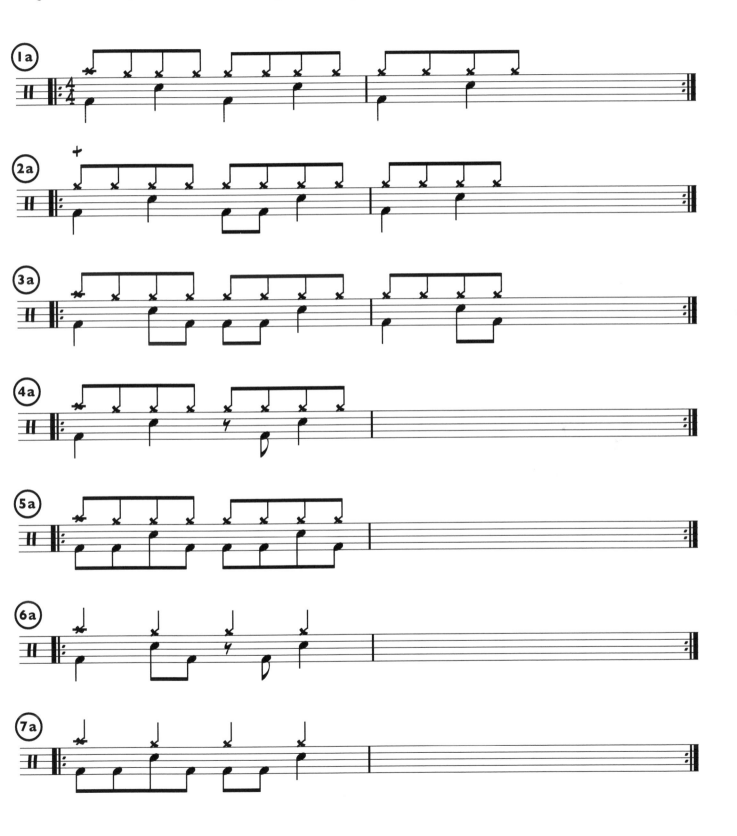

TEACHER'S NOTES - LEVEL 7

"I told people I was a drummer before I even had a set -
I was a mental drummer" - Keith Moon

EIGHTH NOTE TRIPLET STICKING EXERCISES

Beginner - Play each exercise with a gradually increasing tempo

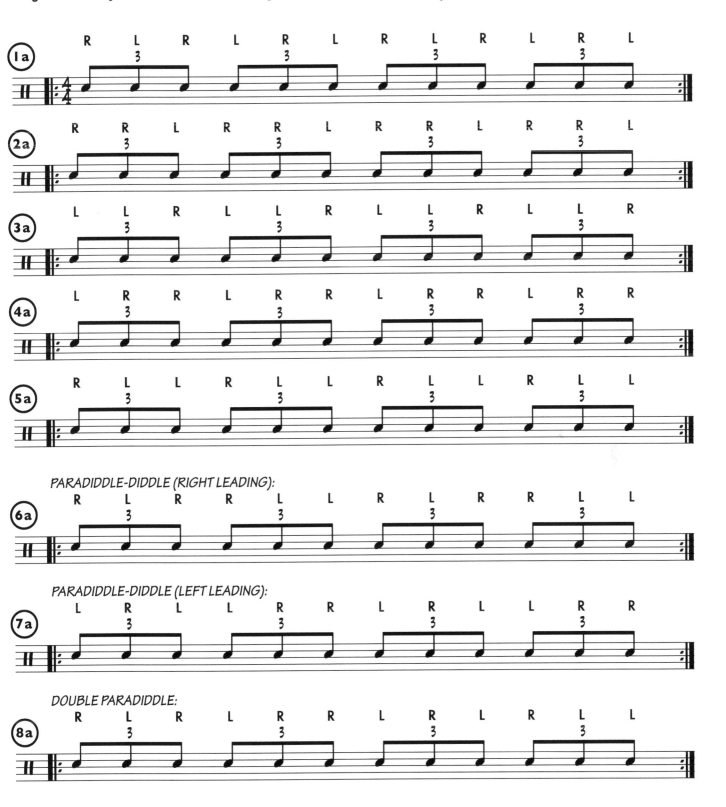

EIGHTH NOTE TRIPLET RHYTHM EXERCISES

Beginner - Play each exercise four times
Advanced - Play all sixteen exercises consecutively without repeats

EIGHTH NOTE TRIPLET BEATS

Beginner - Play each exercise four times

Advanced - Play all fourteen exercises consecutively without repeats

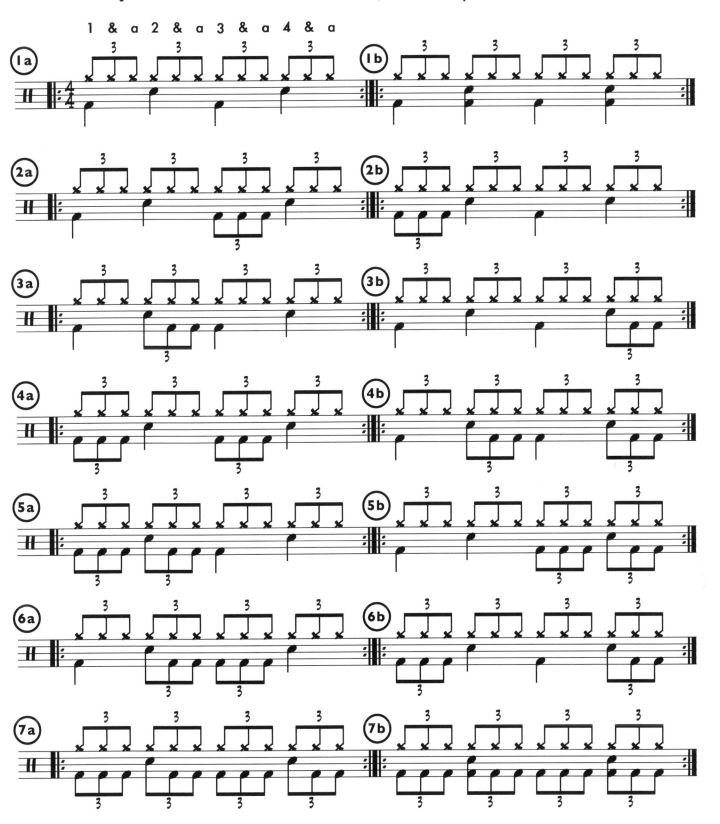

EIGHTH NOTE TRIPLET FILLS

Beginner - Play each exercise four times
Advanced - Play all seven exercises consecutively without repeats

EIGHTH NOTE TRIPLET FILLS: CREATE YOUR OWN

Beginner - With your teacher, create your own eighth note triplet fills using the same beats

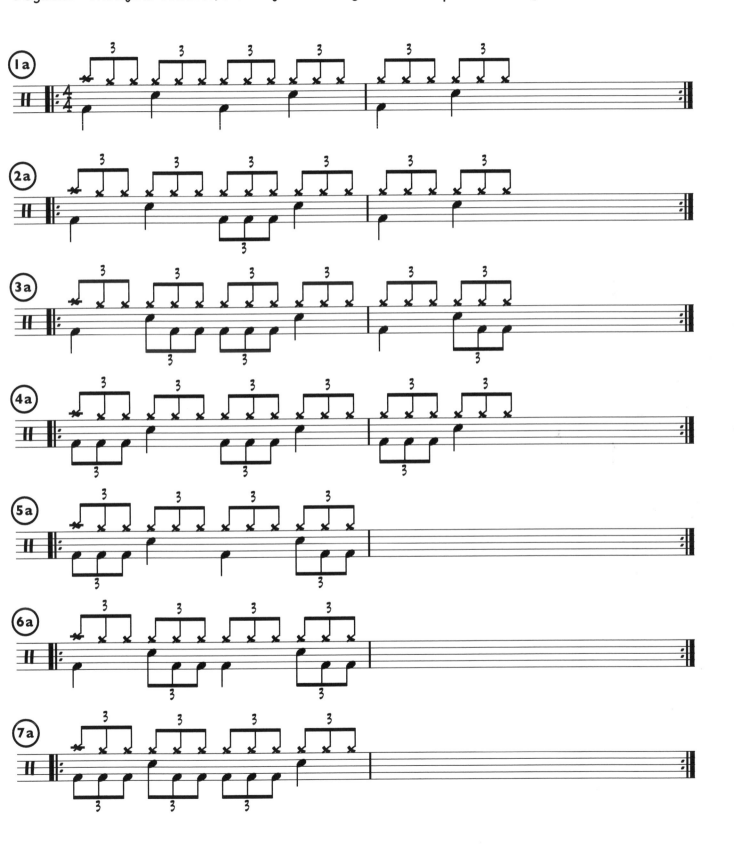

EIGHTH NOTE TRIPLET ENDURANCE EXERCISES

Beginner - Play each exercise as long as possible, gradually increasing the tempo
Advanced - Play all four exercises consecutively without repeats

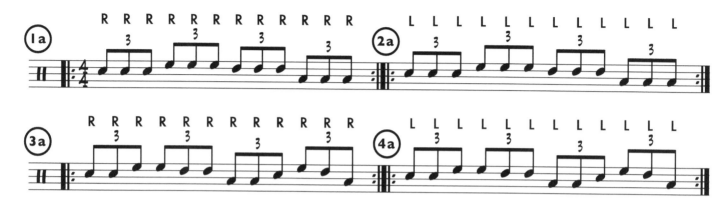

EIGHTH NOTE TRIPLET DRUM SET EXERCISES

Beginner - Play each exercise as long as possible, gradually increasing the tempo
Advanced - Play all eight exercises consecutively without repeats

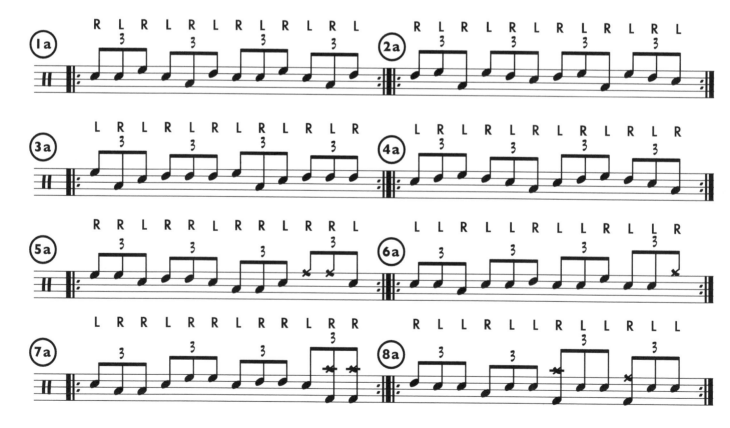

TEACHER'S NOTES - LEVEL 8

"I have to give my family credit for putting up with the racket, because as some of you may know, it's not the easiest thing in the world to live with a kid who's trying to become a Rock 'n' Roll drummer" - Max Weinberg

EIGHTH NOTE SWING TRIPLETS

Beginner - Play each exercise four times
Advanced - Play all sixteen exercises consecutively without repeats

EIGHTH NOTE SWING TRIPLET BEATS

Beginner - Play each exercise four times

Advanced - Play all fourteen exercises consecutively without repeats

EIGHTH NOTE SWING TRIPLET FILLS

Beginner - Play each exercise four times
Advanced - Play all seven exercises consecutively without repeats

SWING TRIPLET FILLS: CREATE YOUR OWN

Beginner - With your teacher, create your own swing triplet fills using the same beats

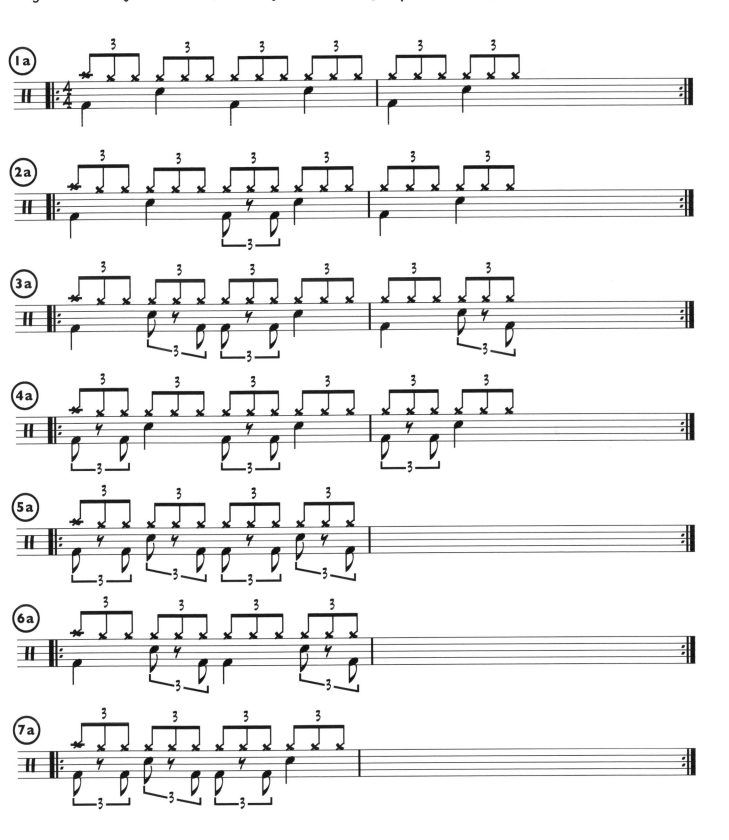

EIGHTH NOTE TRIPLET COMBO BEATS (WITH RIDE)

Beginner - Play each exercise four times
Advanced - Play all seven exercises consecutively without repeats

©2013 Owen Liversidge • Teacher and Student Publications

MUSICAL STYLES: THE BLUES "SHUFFLE" BEAT

Beginner - Play each exercise four times
Advanced - Play all six exercises consecutively without repeats

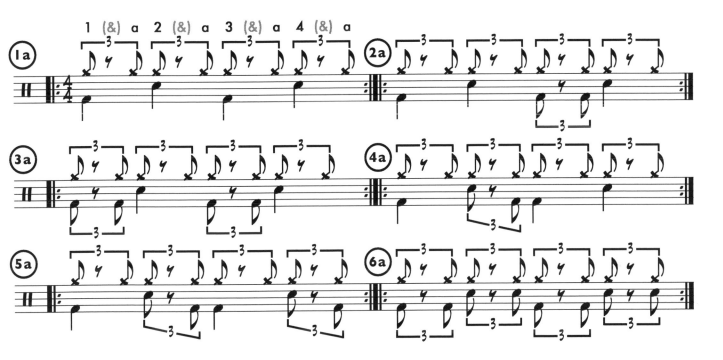

MUSICAL STYLES: THE JAZZ "SWING" BEAT

Beginner - Play each exercise four times
Advanced - Play all six exercises consecutively without repeats

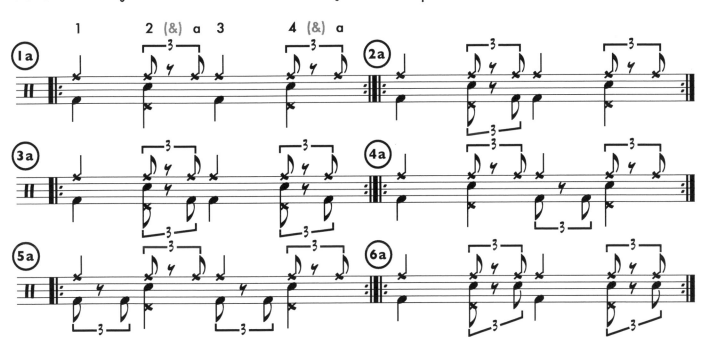

TEACHER'S NOTES - LEVEL 9

"If you just sit there and you know that rule #1 is just that everything you do is honest and just a natural and instinctual extension of your self, then there you go" - Lars Ulrich

ALTERNATING SIXTEENTH NOTE BEATS

Beginner - Play each exercise four times
Advanced - Play all sixteen exercises consecutively without repeats

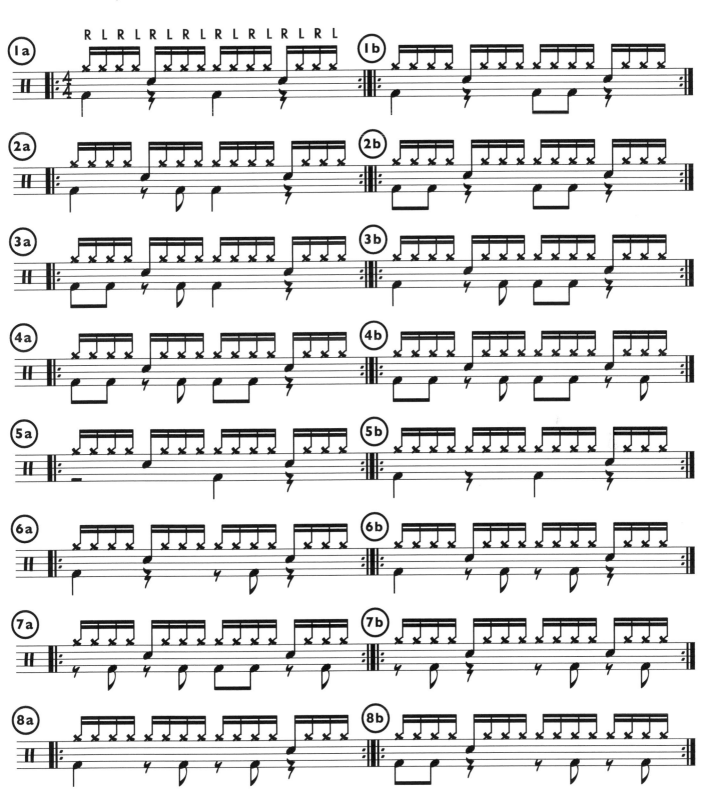

USING BOTH STICKS ON CYMBALS

Beginner - Play each exercise four times, using 2nd crash if available
Advanced - Play all four exercises consecutively without repeats

SIXTEENTH NOTES AND EIGHTH NOTE TRIPLETS

Beginner - Play each exercise four times
Advanced - Play all four exercises consecutively without repeats

ALTERNATING EIGHTH NOTE TRIPLET BEATS

Beginner - Play each exercise four times
Advanced - Play all fourteen exercises consecutively without repeats

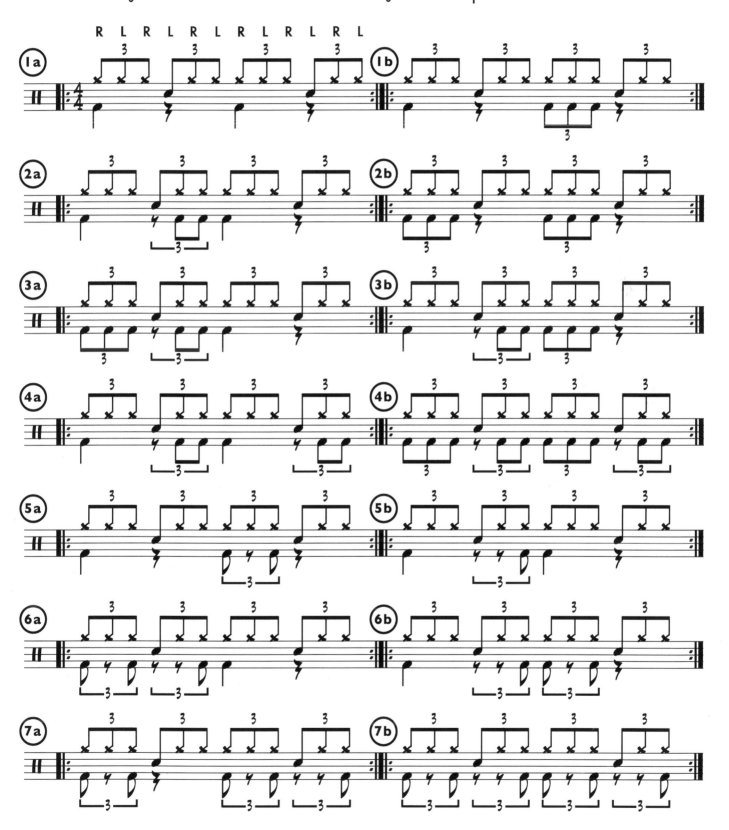

MUSICAL STYLES: ADDITIONAL LATIN GROOVES

Beginner - Play each exercise four times, as examples

ADVANCED NUMBER CELLS

Beginner - Play each fill four times as an example, then create your own on next page
Advanced - Play all six exercises consecutively without repeats

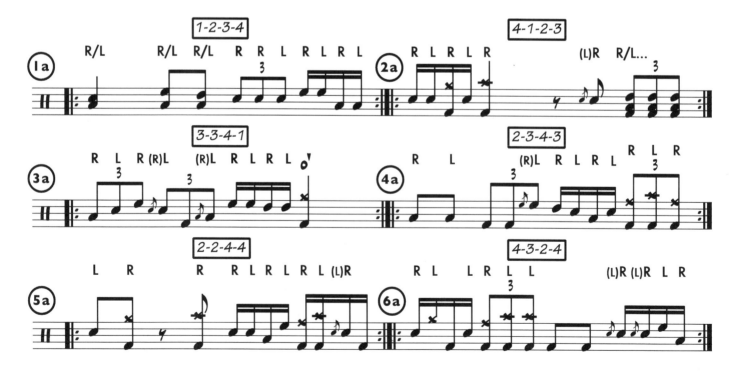

TEACHER'S NOTES - LEVEL 10

"Of course I'm ambitious! What's wrong with that? Otherwise you sleep all day"
- Ringo Starr

*Create your own fills using a chosen number cell

1-4-3-2

EIGHTH NOTE "OFF" BEATS

Beginner - Play each exercise four times
Advanced - Play all sixteen exercises consecutively without repeats

EIGHTH NOTE "OFF" BEATS WITH RESTS

Beginner - Play each exercise four times
Advanced - Play all fourteen exercises consecutively without repeats

EXPLORING THE 2/4 TIME SIGNATURE

Beginner - Play each exercise four times
Advanced - Play both sets of exercises consecutively without repeats

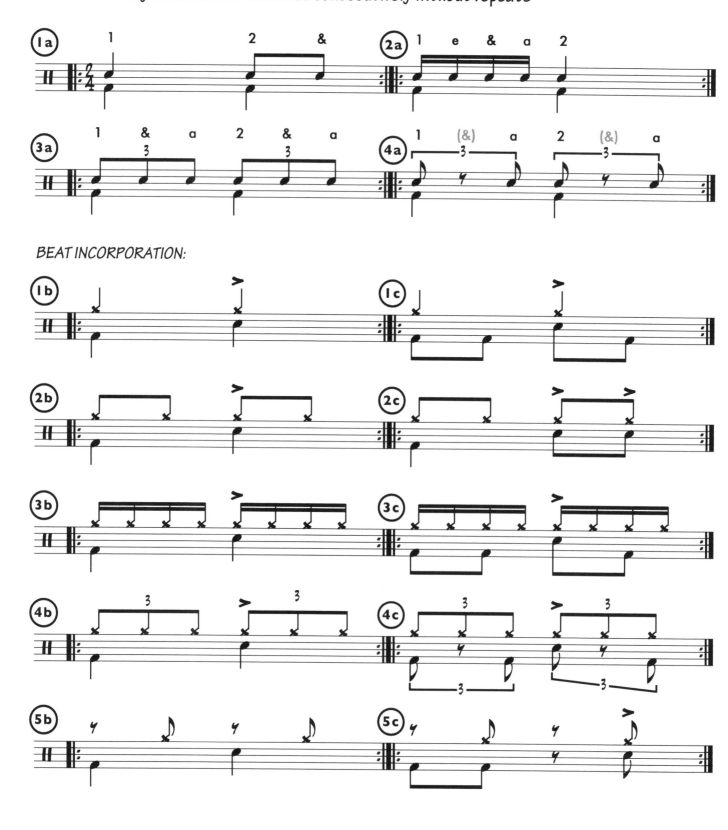

BEAT INCORPORATION:

EXPLORING THE 3/4 TIME SIGNATURE

Beginner - Play each exercise four times
Advanced - Play both sets of exercises consecutively without repeats

BEAT INCORPORATION:

EXPLORING THE 5/4 TIME SIGNATURE

Beginner - Play each exercise four times
Advanced - Play both sets of exercises consecutively without repeats

TEACHER'S NOTES - LEVEL 11

"Drumming was the only thing I was ever good at" - John Bonham

DOTTED NOTE RHYTHM EXERCISES

Beginner - Play each exercise four times
Advanced - Play all sixteen exercises consecutively without repeats

EIGHTH NOTE BEATS WITH DOTTED NOTES

Beginner - Play each exercise four times
Advanced - Play all sixteen exercises consecutively without repeats

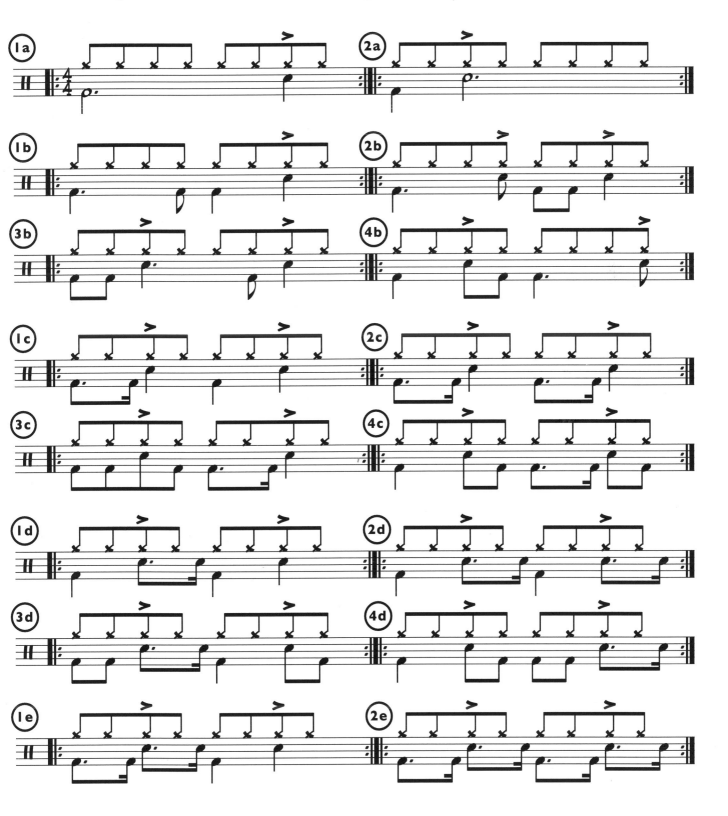

MORE EIGHTH NOTE BEATS WITH DOTTED NOTES

Beginner - Play each exercise four times
Advanced - Play all sixteen exercises consecutively without repeats

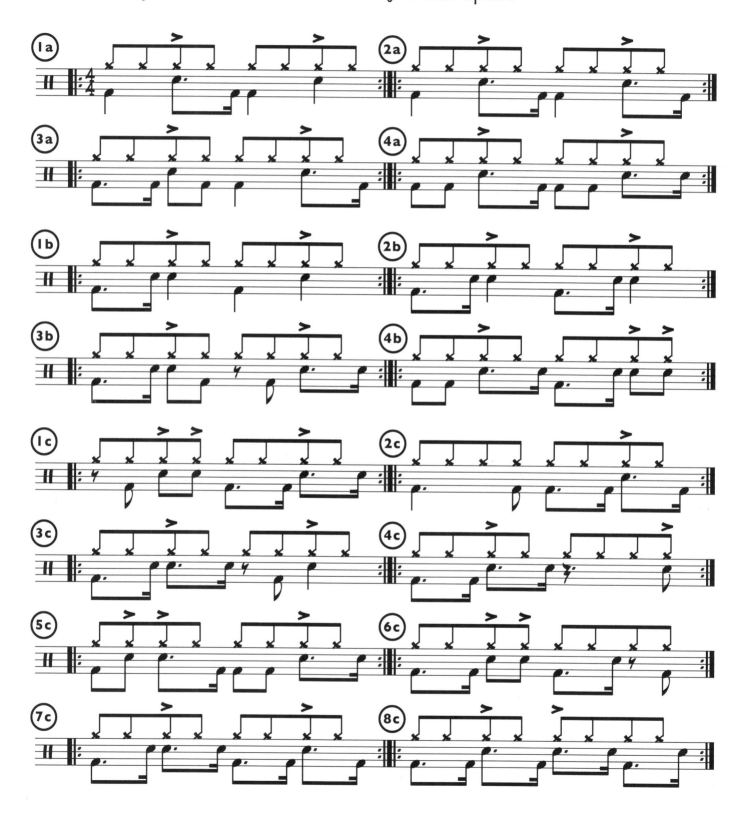

DOTTED EIGHTH NOTE FILLS

Beginner - Play each exercise four times
Advanced - Play all eight exercises consecutively without repeats

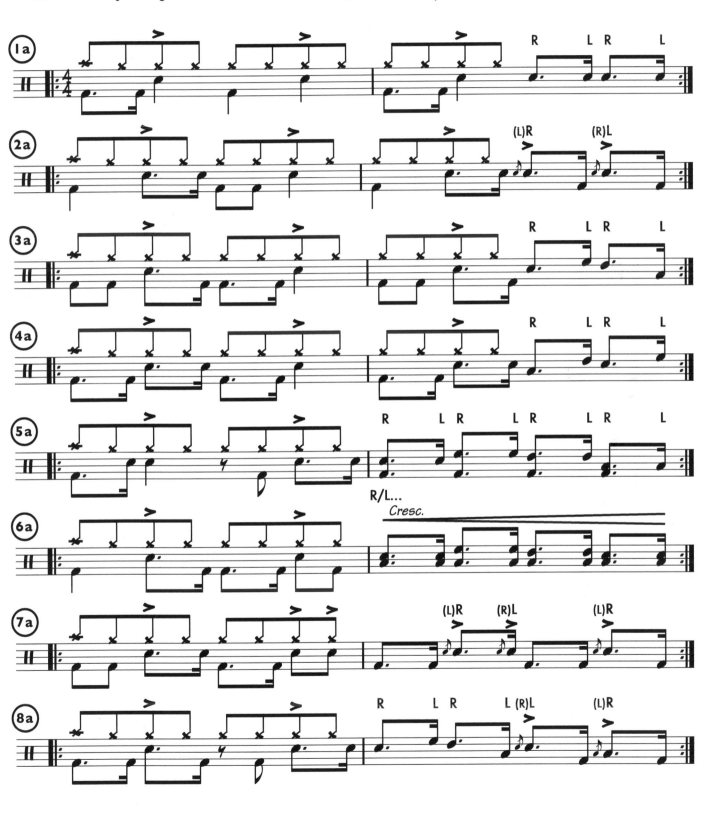

DOTTED EIGHTH NOTE FILLS: CREATE YOUR OWN

Beginner - With your teacher, create your own dotted eighth note fills using the same beats

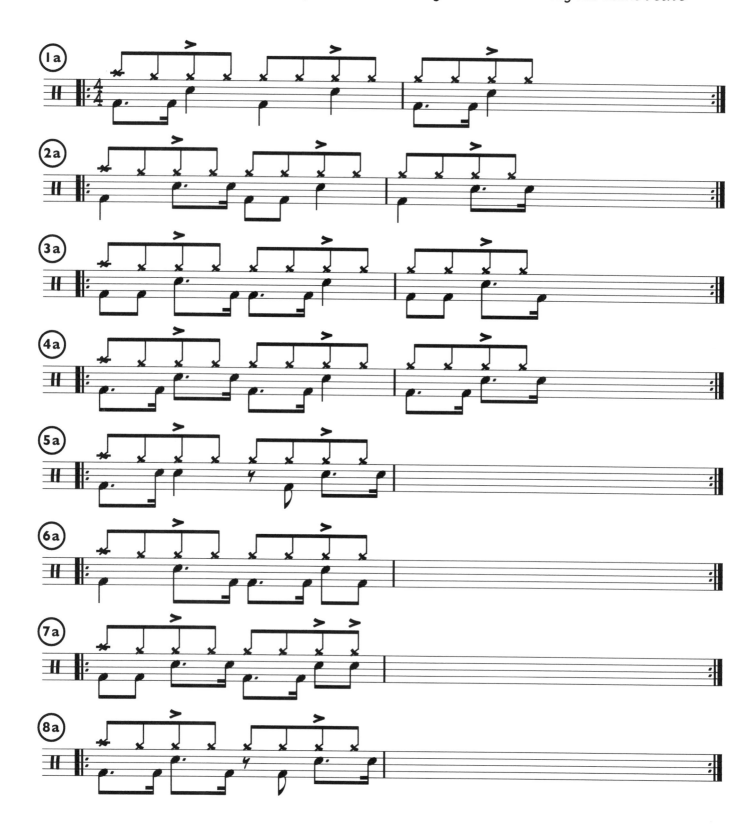

SIXTEENTH NOTE FRAGMENTS

Beginner - Play each exercise eight times
Advanced - Play all twenty four exercises consecutively without repeats

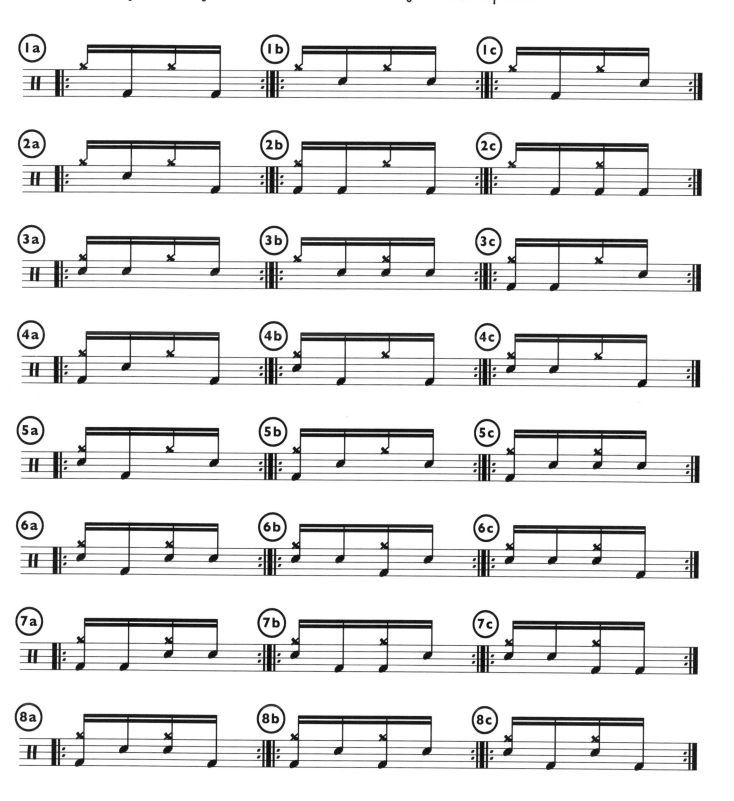

BLANK MANUSCRIPT

BLANK MANUSCRIPT

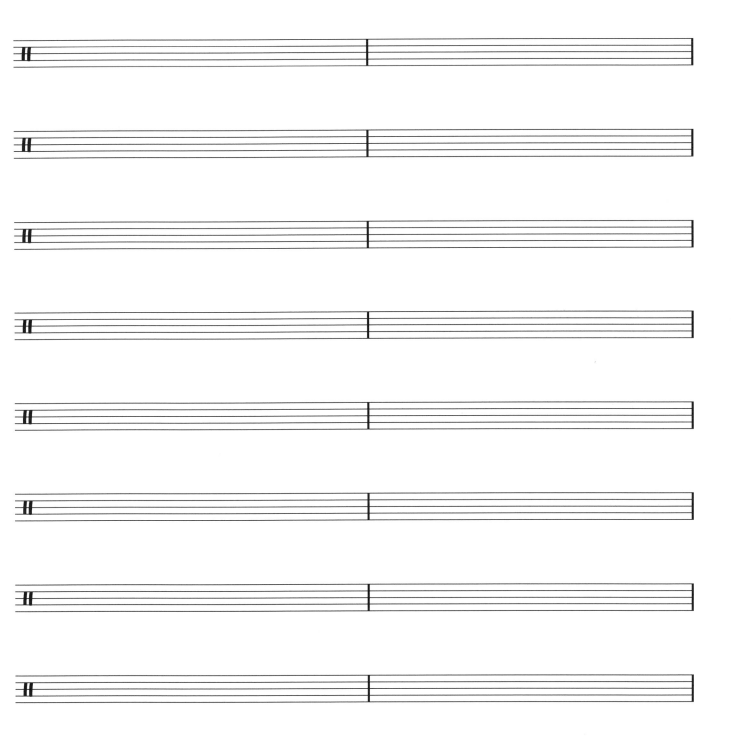

BLANK MANUSCRIPT

BLANK MANUSCRIPT

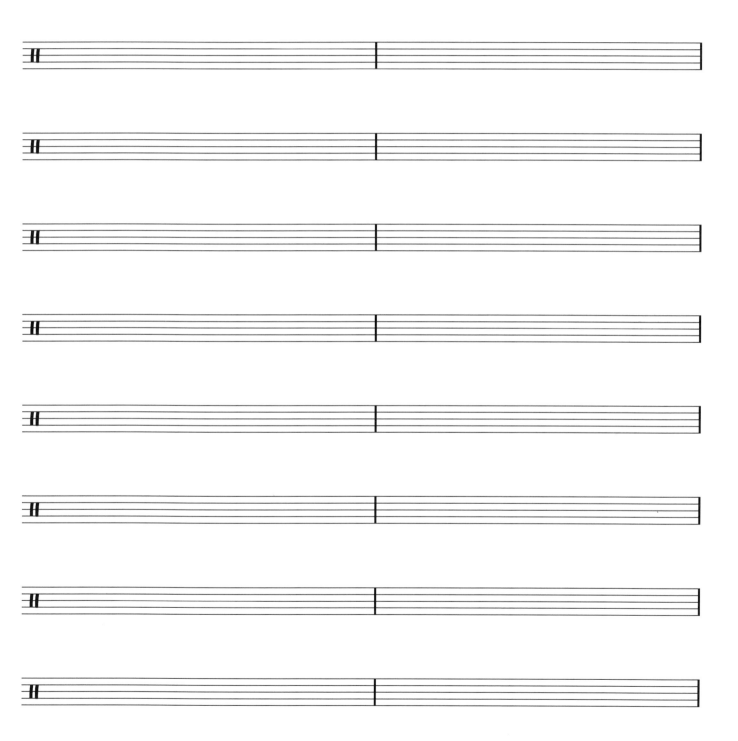

BLANK MANUSCRIPT

CONGRATULATIONS!

You have completed **The Teacher and Student Method Drum Set Studies Exercise Book 1**. Before moving onto **Exercise Book 2**, why not review this book by playing all of the **Advanced** instructions (if you haven't already).

Also available:

The Teacher and Student Method Drum Set Studies Exercise Book 2

Thanks to:

Chris McCaig, Jason Monseur, Leirrie Valentin, Andrew Hill, Andy Ziker, Dan Brigstock, Scott Sanders, and all of my students for being guinea pigs in the making of this book!

teacherandstudentbooks.com